AMERICAN MONEY AND THE FLOW OF ILLEGAL IMMIGRATION ON THE RIO GRANDE

LIFE ON A REMOTE WEST TEXAS RANCH

MY SIMPLE PROPOSAL FOR U.S. IMMIGRATION REFORM

MARIA LUISA MIRANDA

iUNIVERSE, INC.
NEW YORK BLOOMINGTON

American Money and the Flow of Illegal Immigration on the Rio Grande
Life on a Remote West Texas Ranch

iUniverse books may be ordered through booksellers or by contacting:

iUniverse
1663 Liberty Drive
Bloomington, IN 47403
www.iuniverse.com
1-800-Authors (1-800-288-4677)

Because of the dynamic nature of the Internet, any Web addresses or links contained in this book may have changed since publication and may no longer be valid.

ISBN: 978-1-4502-0815-4 (sc)
ISBN: 978-1-4502-0817-8 (dj)
ISBN: 978-1-4502-0816-1 (ebk)

Printed in the United States of America

iUniverse rev. date: 3/11/2010

DEDICATION

I dedicate this book to the late Julian Sanchez II, my eldest brother
and a child of the Rustler Springs Ranch. Julian, whom is missed
very much, was the first born of seven siblings.

1951

CONTENTS

INTRODUCTION

People all over the world are willing to sacrifice every comfort to cross into America illegally and earn American money. When a man crosses into another country illegally, he becomes like a bird flying in a gilded cage or like a shackled prisoner walking among the free. He is embracing illegal freedom, thus robbing himself of real freedom—the freedom yielded by compliance with entry laws and policies. The human need for freedom appeals to people of every age, race, and creed, enabling them to think and act illegally. The daily despair of ongoing poverty; the constant ache of human illness and hunger; and the ruinous, degenerative decay from old age all assist in converting the innocence and simplicity of the human heart. As the daughter of illegal immigrants who raised me on a remote ranch in West Texas, I witnessed their daily despair firsthand. I believe that higher expectations through education can decrease America's illegal-immigration problem.

Maria Luisa Miranda

CHAPTER 1:
PENICILLIN, POR FAVOR

The whistling songs of the west wind, the crisp rustle from the leaves of aged cottonwood trees, and the even trickle of cool spring water all welcomed an arid summer morning at the remote Rustler Springs Ranch in far West Texas.

After two cups of hot coffee and a soft, warm flour tortilla with honey butter, I, Maria Luisa Miranda (or just Lou, as I was known), stepped outside to greet the morning and begin my daily chores.

From the empty horse corrals comes an unknown, quivering voice: "American money! American money!" Slowly, I tiptoed to the faded cedar posts of the corral and peeked over. There, in the midst of the corral, were eight sweaty, emaciated, sunburned, and starving illegal aliens (all male) who had walked hundreds of miles to reach *El Ojito*, or Little Spring.

"Food—we need food," said the man offering American money. "We ran out of food three days back after crossing the Rio Grande. We pay American money for food and drink. Here, take this American money and give us food, *por favor*."

I stood there speechless for a few moments and then explained to him that I had plenty of water and food to share, but I would not take his American money. I don't know which left me speechless: his fluent mastery of English, or his heartbreaking condition.

Immediately, I offered them sweet, cold well water to drink, and I brought some warm tortillas and beans that I had prepared earlier. I had been waiting for the arrival of my husband, who was coming in after a week on another ranch. While this bunch of ravenous souls sat eating under the shade of crooked salt cedar and cottonwood trees, the phrase "American money" danced in my mind.

American money was the reason my husband and I had chosen to live in the West Texas hills on a remote ranch, miles from the nearest town. After all, a steady job is something to appreciate and hold on to, even out here in the desert.

The eight desperate fellows savored the moment. They ate and drank in slow motion, talking very little.

Flashbacks from my childhood entered my mind as I sat there watching them consume every bit of their simple meal. I recalled my own parents' story of crossing the Rio Grande from the state of Coahuila, Mexico. They had crossed the river illegally as newlyweds in the late 1940s, eventually living at this very ranch. Their first three years of married bliss were spent on the same remote West Texas ranch I now lived on, in a tin and cardboard one-room shack that was held together with baling wire. Dust, wind, rain, and snow were all regular guests at the shack.

In January 1954, my family was finally caught by the U.S. Border Patrol and deported to Juarez, Mexico. They were apparently deported under the U.S. Immigration's historical landmark of Operation Wetback, which forced the return of all undocumented immigrants back to Mexico.

In Juarez, at the tender age of twenty, my mother began to experience labor pains for the fourth time in her life. A close family friend promptly accompanied her north across the border, just long enough to deliver her fourth American child: me! I came into this world as Maria Luisa Sanchez at Southwestern General Hospital in El Paso, Texas. Thanks be to God! I could have been a Mexican national living in a Third World country or could have become an illegal alien myself. Just the thought of not being an American citizen like my siblings frightens me. I am the only one of seven siblings who was not born in Pecos, Texas.

The never-ending trail of immigrant tears from gross poverty, illness, and despair that many undocumented immigrants must traverse is not one to be envied. American money entices people to gamble with their lives by illegally crossing the river in Texas or the desert in Arizona. As long as American employers offer American money, the poor and desperate will come. Illegal immigrants usually take whatever wages they can get, with no concern for minimum-wage requirements or health benefits. After all, some American money is better than none.

My family eventually gained legal entry into America and moved back to the ranch. At the time of our deportation, my father was earning less than $200 a month as a ranch laborer.

He was willing to earn meager wages in exchange for the opportunity of a better life in America.

As a child, I suffered the consequences of life in an illegal-immigrant family. During my early toddling years, I was dragged several hundred feet by my father's old ranch truck while he and my mother obliviously engaged in a furious oral altercation. Because of their illegal status, they did not feel comfortable driving me to the closest town for medical treatment. After this very stressful, painful, and unjustified event, they bathed me in warm water and picked rocks and pebbles from my raw, bloody body for weeks.

I have been told that I cried every day, all day long, as my tiny bones adjusted to what would eventually become the rest of my painful life. In their fear and ignorance, my parents did not seek professional medical help for me. They feared accusations of child abuse—or worse. Their greatest fear was of deportation back to their Mexican homeland, where American money would become a faded dream.

Several years later, possibly as a result of the unfortunate dragging accident, I suffered an attack of rheumatic fever for several days. Luckily, a local deputy sheriff drove my mother and I to the hospital. My swollen joints and fever were finally treated by medical professionals for the first and last time during my childhood.

All of my confusion, pain, and suffering might have been avoided if education had been a part of our lives.

We as Americans must share in the duty of educating as many illegal immigrants as possible on legal entry rules and laws, on the benefits of citizenship, and on the consequences of illegal entry, thus protecting our country from soaring costs in our public health-care system, public welfare system, and public school system.

We must set higher expectations for America, the greatest country in the world, and for anyone who wants to come and share our great country. It is our American duty to exemplify and teach integrity, dignity, and responsibility to all immigrants, with liberty and justice for all who enter our great country—whether legally or illegally. (People can be educated behind bars, too.)

After many years as resident aliens, both of my parents became American citizens. My father and mother continued to work at the Rustler Springs Ranch for many years, while my siblings and I studied the environment. These are the most memorable years of my life.

I remember the sound of trickling spring water outside my window at night. I remember catching frogs, tadpoles, and minnows in the cool spring. I remember the tickle of the dragonfly's feet on my nose. I remember the smell of wild celery and the pungent taste of tender, wild watercress. I remember the cattle bellowing in the distance. I remember hunting for tiny arrowheads with my family by the Salt Draw (a dry, grassy creek). I remember the hot earth scorching my little feet. I remember not owning a pair of shoes. I did not like shoes, I remember. Shoes were restricting, confining, blistery little things that took my freedom away. I remember my bloody, stumped toes and the occasional mesquite thorn. I remember hiking into the hills when I was four, accompanied by four of my siblings. I remember crossing the thicket in the arroyo without any shoes. I remember exploring the Tinaja, a stone formation where early Native Americans and cattle rustlers once roamed. I remember the laughter and the tears. I remember the blooms of the desert thistle. I remember Daddy's hat waving in the distance. I remember …

My family continued to live and work at the Rustler Springs Ranch long enough to have two more children (for a total of seven). My father was earning $200 a month when he moved the family to a nearby town so that his children could receive a better education.

As I sat in the shade watching eight hungry men eat the food I had prepared for myself and my husband, I was forced to focus on the here and now.

"What time do you expect your husband to come home?" asked the same man who had been doing all the talking for this tattered group. "I need medical attention, and I need your husband's help. I am very ill. I have chills and need penicillin now! I have American money to pay. *Pinicilina, yo necesito pinicilina ya!*"

"Penicillin?" I repeated. "We don't keep medications out here. All I have is aspirin, if you like. Aspirin may help the chills and the ill feeling."

He did not respond, so I directed the group to the hay barn, where some old Army cots and stacks of fresh, green alfalfa hay offered them a safe place to rest. "We will wait for your husband to return," he finally said and then added, "My name is Marcelo." I bid them a good day and went back inside the bunkhouse with my daughter (an eighteen-month-old toddler) and Millie, her black, curly puppy. I did not feel threatened or intimidated by these eight men in any way. Instead, I felt empathetic.

My husband's old, blue truck finally rolled in during the late evening hours. He was exhausted, hot, hungry, and not thrilled with the presence of company in the barn. He knew most of the men and spoke to them in a friendly tone at first, but became irate and loud when Marcelo made his demands. Marcelo asked my husband to give him a penicillin injection with the same syringe and penicillin that he used on sick livestock! My husband refused, fearing complications. With that, he bid them a good night and asked them to move on the next day.

The smell of fried bacon filled the early morning air. My husband was awake at three thirty the next morning, making coffee and breakfast for himself. He always left the coffee on and enough breakfast for my daughter and I to enjoy. This particular morning, however, he was also very stern with me: "*Oyeme! Dijo mi viejo.* You can feed them a little something if you want—*muy poquito*! Then they have to go!" he said. "Tell them to move on. We cannot help them anymore." He drove off in his old Ford truck and would not return for another week. He was bound for the Dilihunt Ranch. His best horse, Mango, and the *remuda* (working horses) were eagerly awaiting his timely arrival.

My husband's concern with the company in the hay barn was not without good intentions. I was in my first trimester of pregnancy with my second child, out there alone, and he feared someone may try to take advantage of me. However, the *hombres* left early in the morning after a quick breakfast, just as my husband had asked. I did not see them leave. Hung with a piece of baling wire from the latch of the barn door was a paper wad of twenty-five American dollars.

I had been raised around many illegal aliens who had worked for my father, so I did not ever fear or distrust them in any way. Instead, I found their complicated lifestyle interesting. I felt concern for them and always wanted to know more about them—where they stayed and how they lived, whether in tent camps, wet shacks (small, one-room shacks that generally lacked kitchens or bathrooms), abandoned barns, and so on. My father's own complicated life as a ranch hand had lasted many years. Later in life, he was promoted to ranch foreman. He hired *hombres*, (illegal immigrants) as he called them, for all kinds of general ranch labor. I do not condone my father's actions in any way, but now that I'm older, I understand why he hired illegal immigrants: they are a tenacious and hardworking people.

Several of these *hombres* were like family to us. They partook in the care of my siblings and I, often sharing rhymes, games, and songs with us. This was the only life my family and I knew and loved.

Marcelo and his companions were only the first group of illegal aliens I encountered that year. I met thirty-eight desperate men who had braved the illegal journey into America, on foot, in search of that much-needed American money. Although I have been raised among illegal aliens, I do not fully comprehend the suffering and extreme hardships that these determined people exposed themselves to while struggling to acquire American money and a better life. Minimum wage, vacation or health insurance are usually the last items on the priority list of most illegal immigrants. Earning American money is at the top of the list. In their minds, a better life is laced only with American money. These are the rest of their stories.

All the incidents in the following stories occurred in far West Texas during 1973 and 1974.

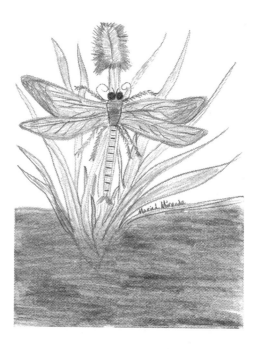

CHAPTER 2:
A SPECK OF RED

The loud roar of the windmill motor was like the sound of a helicopter flying low over the meandering springs. My daughter and I were in the rare company of my industrious husband. He had invited us outside to watch while he dedicated his efforts and undivided attention to the ailing windmill motor. *"Ven y platica con migo afuera,"* dijo mi viejo. *"Pero yo nomas oia el ruido de el papalote rumbando!"*

My husband said, "Please come outside and talk with me." I could only hear the rumbling of the windmill motor.

Little Epis carried an oatmeal can full of colored fish-tank pebbles that she enjoyed decorating the shallow parts of the spring with. With Millie by her side, Epis was allowed to sit, run, splash, and throw pebbles in the cool, clear spring water. She was also allowed to catch a shimmering minnow or hold a tiny tadpole in her eager hands. I even allowed her to munch on watercress and wild celery.

I, on the other hand, sat on the tailgate of our faithful 1968 Ford truck and tried to enjoy the rustling of the cottonwood trees. Suddenly, I noticed a rising cloud of dust in the distance. The cloud advancing on the horizon was like the dust clouds that the horses raised when they raced to the spring for water, except for one thing: I could see a speck of red amid all the dust.

The sight of such a large cloud of dust filled me with a sense of foreboding. What was happening? I turned and spoke to my husband in a loud voice, "Someone is coming! Oh, honey! *Yo miro algo rojo en la distancia. Es una manchita roja en medio de una nube de tierra. La nube viene avanzando rapido, con mucha tierra.* Are you listening to me, honey? *Me estas escuchando viejo? Parece que viene alguien!"* "It looks like someone is coming!"

My husband looked up at me from where he knelt by the tired motor and said, "*Si te escucho, pero lo rojo que miras es el Mango. Son los caballos que vienen a la agua.*"

My husband agreed that something was approaching, but he assured me that it was Mango, his hardworking horse, and the rest of the remuda (or large group of working horses) coming to water.

The speck of red made me doubt his horse theory. Not convinced by his answer, I jumped off the tailgate and moved to a high spot by the spring to get a better look. I had just adjusted my eyes to my new position when suddenly, the dust cloud turned into many human silhouettes moving at a fast pace! I ran to inform my husband, who couldn't hear me because of the roar of the motor. At my insistence, and as the speck of red moved into range, my husband finally stood up to take a closer look.

"That is a large group of men approaching, and one is wearing a red rag around his neck," he said. He groaned. "Go and get the fresh water pail ready, and I will greet them."

I took my daughter by the hand and led her and Millie back to the house. As I was walking, I heard a sound like the sudden rush of many horses galloping to water. I turned to see many men running toward the spring. They confronted the spring much as the horses would: Some dropped to their hands and knees, slurping and splashing. Some flopped on their bellies, sipping, gurgling, and spattering the salty spring water at the same spot where the livestock drank!

Instantly, I called to them, "*No, no tomen agua salada!*" The ten hot, dusty, thirsty *hombres* turned a deaf ear to me as they drank the cool water. So I yelled out in English, "*No, don't drink that salty water. We have fresh water!*" The dusty ten continued to ignore me, focused only on the blue sea before them.

I counted them again. Indeed, there were ten of them—ten more Mexican nationals whose tragedy could be found in their unending cycle of poverty. One was wearing a bright red bandanna around his neck, just as my husband had said.

Once again, these men spoke of the American money to be made in the West Texas oil fields. They were in pursuit of their own oil well—their own American dream. The group still had hard tortillas and jerky in their backpacks but had not had water for two days. "The mountains, the river, and the desert have claimed a lot of our people," the one in the red bandanna said. "We are lucky to have made it this far." I did not ask for further explanation, fearing what his answer might be.

"Now we will have a drink of your fresh water," said one of our dusty, dehydrated guests. My husband sat and talked with them for a while and then directed them to the barn or the shady backyard for a rest. The *hombres* just wanted to get to Orla, so they could call family in Odessa. The Texas oil fields were waiting!

Very early the next morning, my husband left for the ranch in New Mexico, and he did not take any of the ten hombres with him. Their leader had asked him to drop them off in a ravine by a dirt road close to Orla, where they could rest until nightfall. According to their proposed plan, a designated man would walk to Orla after nightfall and call his family in Odessa from a public pay phone.

My husband regretfully did not agree to give them a ride to Orla for fear of losing his job. As he drove off in the cool darkness of the early morning, I heard the men scrambling in the barn. I wondered what their reaction would be toward me at breakfast, but they showed no reaction. They drank coffee, packed their food, and left within the hour, traveling in the same direction as my husband. They would walk to Orla—approximately thirty miles.

Evidently, they had done this before; they had change for the pay phone, which required American money.

When my husband returned from New Mexico that evening, he told me that he would be leaving for the Dilihunt Ranch for eight to ten days. He would leave us with plenty of money, in case my extended family came to visit from Toyah. "Go shopping at Pecos," he said with a smile.

Not surprisingly, as days turned into weeks, not a soul drove down the county road that still runs right in front of this remote place. Sometimes, several weeks would go by before my husband came home. I was in the company of my three loyal dogs and my tiny daughter.

My husband dropped by now and then on his way to another job. I was all alone for long periods of time and had to create my own entertainment. On really hot days, we all got in the spring to splash, play, and cool off—including the dogs. Sometimes I let Epis throw more colored pebbles into the spring. She loved to do this; once they were all in the water, she also enjoyed finding them and putting them back into the Quaker Oats can where I kept them. The different colors of the pebbles fascinated her.

Sometimes, on cool days, I packed a picnic lunch, loaded Epis, Millie, and plenty of water on a red wagon, and went for a long walk with the big dogs leading the way. Once we crossed the west arroyo, the big dogs would hunt for rabbit and other game while Epis, Millie, and I hunted for arrowheads in the flats. The whole area was covered with Native American camps and flint chips in every color and size.

My daughter usually gave out after twenty or thirty minutes of walking, so I would put her down in the red wagon for a much-needed nap. I rigged her red wagon with an old umbrella to provide some shade from the sun. Her loyal friend Millie often jumped on the wagon and rested at the feet of her tiny, slumbering mistress.

After several hours of arrowhead hunting, we would head home. On the way, I sometimes thought about the speck of red, the pay phone, and the West Texas oil fields. My husband and I did not hear from the dehydrated ten until three years later, when we moved to Kermit, Texas.

CHAPTER 3:
JUSTO WHISTLES A TUNE

One cloudy day after coming in from our walk, I bathed my daughter and put her and her curly, black companion down for an afternoon nap. As they slept, I took a quick bath and fixed myself a cold glass of iced tea. As I stood there staring out the back window, listening to the wind, I heard a melody coming from the stables of the large, red hay barn. Someone was whistling a tune! Who was there? Other than the three dogs, my daughter and I had been alone for weeks.

I put my shoes on and went outside to see for myself. As I approached the barn, I spotted a short, frail man standing in the corral, unsaddling his horse. "Excuse me. Can I help you?" I asked in English. Then I repeated the question in Spanish: "*Perdone, le podia ayudar con algo?*"

The frail man turned around, and I could not believe my eyes. I tried hard not to stare or to express fear or emotion. I recognized him as a man named Justo, but just barely: His whole face was covered with large, red insect bites and festering blisters that appeared to be infected. The man had so many bites on his face that one of his eyes had swelled shut. His face was oozing and surely very painful, yet he found the strength within himself to whistle a jubilant tune.

"*Buenas tardes,*" said the man. "*Esta su esposo?*" ("Good afternoon. Is your husband here?") I quickly informed him that my husband was at headquarters and was expected to come home soon.

"I have been living alone at the Twin Caves Ranch and have been without food and supplies for a while now," he said. "I rode here on horseback to see if anyone was living here and would share food and medicine with me. I am hungry and need medicine for my face. My boss has not come for almost two months. He was supposed to bring food, medicine, money, and blankets, but he never returned. I need help. I have been surviving on canned tomatoes and black coffee, but now I'm out of canned tomatoes, and I have nothing left to eat." He appeared anxious, in a lot of pain, and very hungry.

I offered him and his tired, sweaty horse a fresh drink of water. I also fixed him a glass of iced tea. While I prepared a bite to eat, he continued to tell me of how he had been eating canned tomatoes for days, sleeping on the rotting wooden floor of the decrepit Twin Caves Ranch house, and using an old mattress for cover at night, because he did not have any beds or blankets. That must have been quite uncomfortable, as the temperature in the desert could drop quite low at night.

While he slept, insects or spiders would bite him on the face. "I have bites all over my body, but it is my face that has the most bites," he willingly informed me. "I feel like my face is on fire." Most likely, red and black bloodsucker insects (from bats and rats) were feeding off this poor man, I thought.

Late that evening, I heard the blaring roar of my husband's truck coming down the dusty west road. The weary blue truck itself sounded anxious to get home. Justo met my husband at the gate; they shook hands and shared a smoke before coming in for supper. We were both appalled at the condition of our acquaintance.

We were glad to have him as a guest at the bunkhouse and were determined to help him any way possible.

Justo was one of the last true cowboys—an honest and hardworking man. He deserved to be fed as promised and be paid an income for services rendered. I had a plan!

After Justo cleaned his face for the second time and doctored it with my daughter's new diaper-rash ointment, he sat down with us to eat supper. He rolled one tortilla with butter and ate it and then rolled another.

After eating his second tortilla, he mixed peanut butter with honey and ate it with tortilla number three!

"Aren't you going to eat supper?" asked my husband. Justo's plate of fried potatoes, refried beans, and *fideos con carne (vermicelli with hamburger)* had not yet been touched. "I have been craving tortillas with butter," he said with a tortured smile.

Finally, he proceeded to eat his supper. He ate slowly and ingested every tasty morsel on his plate. Later, he followed my husband outside for another cigarette.

Justo remained with us for several days; he needed time to heal from the insect bites on his aging face. Days later, my husband drove Justo to his own headquarters, so he could get some assistance and maybe some well-deserved and well-earned greenbacks.

I took it upon myself to write his boss a note in English; my husband would deliver it. I reminded Justo's boss of fair-labor laws, human decency, and respect toward our fellow man. His boss paid him promptly and gave Justo an ointment for his face. Justo continued to whistle jovial tunes and work at surrounding ranches for many years.

Maria Luisa Miranda

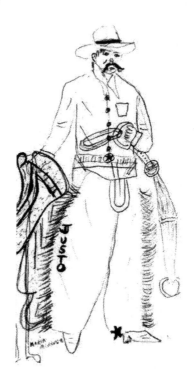

CHAPTER 4:
NIGHT RIDERS

Even after late autumn arrived, the human migration continued, although at a slower pace. My husband said it would pick up again after the winter season. "Most of the people who wanted to cross over are already here," he informed me. "The rest will follow in late winter or early spring."

I encountered twenty-three travelers in two months, and not once did I see the U.S. Border Patrol—not by van, jeep, helicopter, or horseback. I wondered whether they patrolled this far from the border (approx. 130 miles).

In 1954, the U.S. Border Patrol, acting apparently under Operation Wetback, had arrested and deported my family (including three toddlers) when we lived at this very place. Yet in 1973, some nineteen years later, the Border Patrol was nowhere to be found. It appeared as if though illegal immigration was not at the top of anyone's agenda that year.

I didn't have any more visitors until late November, when four famished *hombres* arrived at the spring. They became distraught upon realizing that a family was living there once again: "Senora, what are you doing here? It is very dangerous here. You must leave this place immediately!"

I was baffled by their illogical behavior. I did not understand the fear in their frantic eyes. I had never had an experience such as this, so I did not know how to react. They began to murmur frantically among themselves. I stood quietly and stared.

Eventually, I tried to reassure them that this was a very safe place to raise a family. In fact, this was the second time I had had the privilege of living at this remote place. How and why would I fear the place I knew and loved as my home? The Rustler Springs Ranch was and is the love of my life—for all of my life.

The fearful four would not even go to the hay barn to rest; they insisted on resting by the elder salt cedar trees that embraced the eastern trail of the spring. "We want to be able to see," claimed the dread-filled four.

That evening, I made refried beans and *fideos again* (vermicelli) for supper and invited my four guests in to eat. They declined my offer to come in, instead selecting a clearing outside beneath the swaying trees. So Epis, Millie, and I joined them. I wanted to know more. What was it about the Rustler that frightened them? What had happened here that made them so leery?

After formal introductions, I asked the speaker of the group, a man named Jesus, to tell me their story.

He began by saying that a few years back, he had worked at the Rustler Springs Ranch. At night, he claimed, strange things began to happen.

This piqued my curiosity, so I said, "More—tell me more, please!"

First, he recalled how he and his *companeros* had heard "*fantasmas gritando y jinetes a caballo en la noche oscura.*" He claimed many phantom riders ran past, yelling and galloping their horses at a fast pace, like ghost riders in the night.

"They rode the path between the spring and the house," said Jesus in a trembling voice. "They appeared to be dragging chains, or at least it sounded like chains. I guess it could have been something else. It could have been money. It could have been hundreds of coins jingling … maybe gold coins."

"Gold coins?" I asked. "You're afraid of gold coins?"

One of the other hombres responded, "We don't fear the gold coins. We're afraid of the devilish phantoms that ride the wild horses in the night. We're afraid to go outside, because we might get trampled by these night riders. Their steeds are angry, and they gallop madly."

As I sat there, eating and listening, I tried to keep an open mind; after all, most Mexican people (including myself) are somewhat superstitious. I wanted to believe … but night riders, really? Why hadn't these night riders graced me with their presence?

"There are other things that happen here at night," said Jesus as he stood up to leave. "We are not staying here tonight. We will walk to the Paloma Ranch next door and stay there. May God be with you, ma'am."

As Jesus and his *companeros* set out on their three-mile hike, I reminded them that no one lived at Paloma Ranch. It was one of the ranches that my husband looked after. Jesus and his men did not seem concerned; they were determined to spend the night anywhere but at Rustler Springs. In the morning, they would continue their journey east in search of American money.

I wondered if Jesus and his friends would accept wages in *monedas de oro Americano*—or American gold coins.

CHAPTER 5:
HUMBERTO AND THE BLACK WILD COWS

A few days later, I was harboring that unattractive feeling that everyone knows: feeling too fat, too old, and too tired. So I decided to enhance my femininity and desirability.

My husband had been gone for days. I longed for the sound of his voice; his warm, soothing touch; and his strong embrace. I was ready for my man to come home.

That evening, after rinsing and soaking a large basket of cotton diapers by hand—and after Epis, my daughter (whose real name is Sharon Michelle), had fallen asleep—I took action. I wasn't going to let a basket of dirty diapers get me down! I took a cold bath, sprinkled my body with perfumed talc, and put bright red ribbons in my long, dark, silky hair. Then I put my bright red, very snug baby-doll pajamas on my unshapely pregnant body. (Red was my husband's favorite color). Then I went to bed. I felt pretty all night long! *Maybe he'll come home tonight*, I thought.

The next morning, after listening to the soft wind blow, I put on my red house slippers and went to hang diapers on the line before my daughter awoke. She was a very curious child, and I was afraid that she might slip and fall on the muddy banks of the deep spring, as I had done so many years before.

I picked up my basket of wet diapers and wobbled outside. I found both Cinnamon and Barker lying by the door, wagging their tails as if to say, "We've been waiting for you."

I said to them, "Come on, y'all. Let's go hang some diapers."

As I went around the corner of the house on my way to the clothesline, I heard a man's deep voice say, *"Buenos dias."* I stopped cold in my tracks and could not see anyone until a slightly gray-haired man sat up in the middle of the field of toboso grass (a type of wild grass found in West Texas) that surrounded our bunkhouse. *"Buenos dias,"* he repeated. *"De donde vienes y que haces hay en el sacaton?" yo le preguntaba.*

"Porque los perros no ladraron? Quien eres y que quieres?"

"Where did you come from and what are you doing there in the tall grass?" I asked. "Why didn't the dogs bark? Who are you, and what do you want?" I asked in a rude and frightened voice. I was enduring the element of surprise.

Suddenly, I was appalled at myself—stunned by my own ignorance and embarrassed by my stupidity. I was still wearing my bright red, snug baby-doll pajamas, and there was nowhere to hide! I wasn't feeling very pretty now, so I yelled at my newest visitor, advising him to sit still while I went inside to get dressed.

"Aqui la esperamos," the man said. ("We will wait for you here.") *We?* This meant he was not alone!

So I asked, *"La esperamos? Usted y quien mas?"* (You and who else?)

Out from the toboso grass resounded, *"Buenos dias." "Buenos dias." "Buenos dias." "Buenos dias." "Buenos dias." "Buenos dias."*

Seven men had walked into our yard in the night and were sleeping by the spring in the tall field of toboso grass! Barker and

Cinnamon's canine faces appeared to smile; they were pleased to have company once again. I was losing confidence in my supposedly fierce watchdogs. They had been brought to the ranch by a friend who described them as some of the meanest and the best in the watchdog business.

"Remember, they are man's best friend," she had said. "They will protect you." She was right about one thing: They were man's best friend ... every man's best friend! There were no strangers among them!

I stepped back slowly with the cold, dripping basket of diapers in front of my protruding four-month belly and kept a steady eye on the *hombre* in the grass. When I got to the door, I dropped the basket of diapers and ran in the house, locking the door behind me. It didn't take me but a few minutes to get dressed. I was now in a somewhat frightened and hyper mood.

After I composed myself, I went back outside, only to find that the diaper basket was gone. I walked slowly around the side of the house ... and there they were! Hanging neatly, side by side on the sunniest area of the clothesline, were my daughter's diapers. They created a beautiful line of white, wispy clouds that looked like something out of a modern-day photographic magazine. I could not see the *hombres* but could hear their voices farther down the stream, so I slowly and cautiously followed their voices. I was not prepared for what came next.

One of the men, a young man of seventeen years, had left his beloved Mexico wearing nothing on his feet but a pair of *huaraches* (leather sandals).

Along the trail, sharp crags of volcanic rock; needle-like thorns from mesquite brush and prickly cacti; and blistering friction from the shoes themselves had turned his two exhausted feet into bloody masses of aching human flesh. His *companeros* had gathered around him, trying to soak his feet in the cool, salty spring water. This didn't do his raw feet any favors! The young man was wailing like a lone coyote or like a lost child who can't find his mother. His painful cries startled me. I had never heard a man cry like this before. I was at a loss for words.

"*Necesita medicina*," said the man I had spoken to earlier. ("He needs medicine.")

"*Bueno*," I said. I waddled quickly to the house to look for anything that might help. I was so limited in supplies that the only items I could find were aspirin and a jar of petroleum jelly. I kept petroleum jelly for my daughter's diaper rash and had plenty on hand. I quickly tore an old, white cotton sheet into large strips and gathered my *medicina*. Then I heard my daughter ask, "*Porque ta Gelio llorando*, Mama?" ("Why is Gelio crying, mama?")

Rogelio was a young illegal immigrant man who worked for my dad. The wailing in the backyard had apparently awoken her. She was standing on her bed with her face pressed against the window screen, looking concerned. My daughter was very fond of Gelio.

"*El tiene coco*," I said. "*Hay estese mija y no se baje de la cama*." ("Stay there, *mija*, and don't get off the bed.") I wobbled outside as fast as I could.

I offered my *medicina* to the *hombres*, and they quickly dried the young man's feet, applied a generous helping of petroleum jelly, and wrapped them gently in fresh, clean cotton cloth.

He politely refused a dose of aspirin, like the famished *hombres* who had come before him. (Many of the Mexican nationals that I met that year turned down American medication for fear of getting sicker.) Several of the other young men carried the wounded soldier to the shade of a waiting cottonwood tree and laid him down to rest.

My toddling daughter had found her way outside and was eagerly waiting to see Gelio. She squatted down beside her brave Gelio, staring inquisitively into his eyes for an answer.

Up until this time, the *hombres* and I had not had time for formal introductions. The older man's name was Humberto, and the six young men traveling with him were his two sons and four nephews. The young men had heard tales of American money. They had been so enticed by the *plata Americana* that four days earlier that they had made the decision to illegally cross the Rio Grande, dare the mountains near El Paso, and trek the sweltering Chihuahuan desert in search of American money.

Humberto had warned his nephew about making the hazardous journey in *huaraches*, but to no avail. The youngster was on a quest for American money. Nothing would hold him back—not even his leather *huaraches*! Now he lay there writhing, bleeding, and wailing under a cottonwood tree. *Is this really the beginning of a better life?* I wondered.

Later that evening, Humberto made the other five young men help me with supper. "You peel the potatoes," he directed, pointing at each young man in turn. "You make the tortillas. You refry the beans. You will wash the dishes, and you get ready to sweep the kitchen floor." I told him that this was not necessary, but he wouldn't have it any other way. He informed me that he knew my husband well and did not want him to be upset with their presence. He also asked permission to stay a couple of days so that his nephew could heal from the wounds on his feet.

"We won't stay for free," he said in a promising Spanish tone. "We will help you with chores. Just tell me what you need. We will do it for you. Anything—we will do anything if you let us stay." Of course I was going to let them stay a day or two to get their young man back on his feet. That was the only humane thing to do.

The next day, the *hombres* completed a fence that my husband had initiated, painted the newly constructed fence and some gates, pruned all the gnarled cedars by the back door, carried out the trash, fed the old horse in the pen, raked the yard, cleaned out the barn, and asked if there was anything else they could do.

"Well," I said, "There is something else that our boss asked my husband to do, but because of his work overload, he has not been able to do it. There are six wild, young black cows in the front pasture that need to be penned by Friday. Our boss will come again on Friday to pick them up. They have been sold, but we have been unable to pen them. They are very wild! I have tried to pen them with feed, as my husband asked, but was not successful. Before I reached the gate, they became spooked at the noise and ran away once more."

"Oh, we can do that for you. We will pen them for you today," Humberto said with a tone of confidence.

"You don't understand, Humberto. These *vaquillas* (young cows) have always been wild. They do not trust man, and I have no horses available for you to go and get them."

Humberto looked at me with a warm, reassuring smile on his confident, manly face.

"*Nosotros las traemos, senora. Por favor no se preocupe,*" he repeated. ("We will bring them in. Please don't worry.") Humberto and the other five men walked off in the direction of the west *trampita* (west pasture). The injured *hombre* was still resting his aching feet in the hay barn; Humberto instructed him to throw out some fresh hay for the *vaquillas ladinas*, to help settle them down upon arriving at the holding pen.

I stood at the west window and watched the *hombres* disappear over the horizon. It was already after 6:00 PM. *These men have no idea what they are up against,* I thought. *It will be dark soon, and they will probably never find the* vaquillas, *much less pen them.*

I took my daughter in my arms and prepared her nightly bubble bath. I sat and watched her as she played with her yellow rubber duck and other toys. She was pouring water over her head with her favorite pink plastic cup when I heard a loud commotion outside.

I hurried and dried the sudsy toddler, put a clean diaper on her, gave her a bottle of fresh milk, and put her to bed by the west window, so that she could see me outside. "Stay there, *mija*," I said. "I'm going to investigate the noise outside."

I stepped outside and could not believe my eyes. There, in the pen, were the six black *ladinas*, huffing, snorting, foaming at the mouth, charging at the gate, and running around and around in a circle. Humberto and his teenage crew had done it!

Humberto pushed the *vaquillas* toward the fresh hay, but they refused it and just kept butting the fence and gate, looking for a way out. It took the *vaquillas* over an hour to settle down and accept their untimely fate; it took me at least two hours to stop smiling.

Humberto and his staff of young cowboys came by to say good night around eight thirty that evening. I gave them chorizo and potato burritos to take to the barn and share. But first, I asked Humberto what his secret had been in catching the wild *vaquillas*. "How did you catch them so quickly?" I asked.

Humberto quickly explained that cattle do not have good eyesight at night and spook easily. The *hombres* had found them, surrounded them, and spooked them in the direction of the pens, and the *vaquillas* had done the rest. The cows had run straight into the pens for shelter. Two of the young men had run with them and then closed the gate before the *ladinas* had a chance to react.

"*Hay tiene, senora*," said Humberto. ("There you go, ma'am.") Then he bid me a *buenas noches* and left. I had forgotten that most of these *hombres* were used to walking long distances, sometimes without food and water—of course they would accomplish the task! *Both my husband and his boss will be elated*, I thought!

At approximately 11:45 PM that same windy night, I was awoken by a tap on the door. I listened for barking dogs but heard nothing. "Who is it?" I asked.

"*Soy yo, senora*," said Humberto nervously.

I kept four loaded rifles in the house: one by my bed, one by the back door, one by the front door, and one by the west window. All were hidden and out of sight. But when I heard the tremble of fear in Humberto's voice, I just opened the door to see what he wanted at that late hour.

"*Que paso, Humberto?*" I asked.

"*Senora, parece que viene La Migra! Hay viene La Migra!.*"

"Border Patrol, at midnight? Surely not," I responded.

I quickly instructed Humberto to take his men and hide on the top level of the hay barn. I also informed him of a *gringo* who had been annoying me for weeks now. The *gringo* had requested a date with me, even though he knew that I was pregnant and spoken for. I ran him off each time, but he just kept coming, late at night. This was a man who would not take no for an answer.

One night, the drunken *gringo* had tried to tell me that my husband sent him! "Your husband said to come see you. He said for you to let me in. It's all right, honey. He already knows. We're good friends; I've known him for a long time. Now, let me in, or I will let myself in, damn it!"

I stood there quietly for a few seconds, pressing hard against the door. Then I said, "If you can tell me my husband's full name, I will let you in. Otherwise, you need to leave!"

"I can't remember his name; it's one of those Mexican names. I just can't remember, honey, but I promise that he is my friend," said the hopeful drunk.

There was nothing else for me to do; I had to protect myself and my daughter. I instructed him to listen very carefully while I cocked the shotgun close to the door, so he could hear the click.

"If you insist on coming in, I will kill you!" I yelled in a loud and frightened voice.

"Why do you have to be this way?" he had yelled back. "I'll be back, and I am going to get in!" Then he walked quickly to his red and white worn out truck and drove away.

I was determined to keep this man away from me and my daughter. I told Humberto that I would try my best to keep the *Migra* (Border Patrol) from taking him and his family away. But I made him promise that he and his men would protect me if our visitor turned out to be the *gringo* in a red and white pickup: "Listen for my cue and come quickly, Humberto. Please promise! *Si es un gringo en una camioneta roja con blanca me ayudas, Humberto, por favor! Ven pronto!*"

"Please do not worry. I will kill him for you," he said gently and then sped off into the night. Speechless, I quickly locked the door and prepared to meet the midnight traveler.

My heart skipped a beat as I rushed to put on jeans and a shirt and get my rifles into position. I turned off all lanterns, checked on my daughter and Millie (the puppy), made sure the back door was locked, and crept slowly outside with a loaded shotgun to get a better look around and to listen for familiar sounds. In the distance, by the fish ponds, I could see the headlights coming. I could hear the roar of the vehicle's motor as it came closer and closer. I wondered if Humberto and his boys were as nervous as I was. My heart pounded in my chest, and the cool air chilled my sweaty brow and hands.

Often, I sat outside late at night with the dogs and listened to the sounds of the night. I was familiar with and could distinguish several different truck sounds and most animal sounds, both tame and wild. This was one of my favorite things to do after dark. I had no television, no radio, no electricity, limited material to read—and most of the time, no husband. He was married to his job, and because it was said that he could do the job of five men, he kept very busy. It was almost time for him to come home, though, if only for a day.

When the vehicle approached the gate that led into the ranch, I listened carefully to see if I could recognize it. *That sounds like Daddy's truck*, I thought. Then I thought I heard my daddy's voice as he greeted those who were always ready to welcome traveling strangers, even at midnight! Barker and Cinnamon ran in front of the truck as he arrived at the house, serving as his welcoming committee. It was Daddy!

I ran to him, gave him a hug, and asked what he was doing out so late. He lived two counties away, across the hills, and it was not like him to be out this late at night on a weekday. Almost struggling for breath, he said, "I'm going to work cattle, and I don't have any *hombres* to help me. All I have is two neighbors. I need hands. Is your man here? Does he have any available men who can help? Do you know, *mija*? I really need his help."

By "work cattle," my father was referring to the process by which he gathered with a roundup, cut, branded, and shipped cattle. He had come here at night in order to avoid Border Patrol. I told Daddy that my husband would not be back for a few days. He advised me that he did not have a few days to spare; he would begin shipping in a few days! Daddy walked to the back of his pickup and unloaded a huge watermelon. "This is for you and Epis," he said.

I could see the frustration building on his tired, gray, wrinkled brow. So I said, "I may have a solution for you, Daddy." Then I yelled, "Humberto, *venga!*"

As Humberto walked out of the darkness, my frustrated daddy said, "Oh, this is good, but I'm in need of several men!"

I introduced them formally first; then I said to Humberto, "Daddy is looking for hands. Do you think you can help him? He is looking for several cowboys to help him work cattle."

That same reassuring smile that I had seen earlier on Humberto's handsome weathered face reappeared. He threw his head back and yelled, "*Muchachos, vengan!*" I'll never forget the look on my daddy's face as he stood there in awe. First, three of the *muchachos* walked out of the darkness and greeted my dad by shaking his hand. A few steps behind them trailed the other two, carrying their injured cousin, whose name I never did know. Daddy's expression changed from one of frustration to one of relief.

"*Buenas noches, senor,*" said the young men in tangled voices.

"*Buenas noches muchachos,*" replied Daddy. After that, he gratefully yelled, "*Quien quiere trabajar?*" ("Who wants to work?")

"*Nosotros!*" several of them responded with joy. ("All of us!")

Daddy stared at the injured young man for a minute; he had remained silent. "You can work too, you dummy," he declared.

"You can be our camp cook!" My dad was a bit harsh, but he meant well. I felt that this unusual situation was just meant to be: the *hombres* were looking for work, and my father desperately needed their help. They all hugged and talked and expressed their joy for a few minutes. Then my daddy asked, "*Quien quiere sandia?*" ("Who wants watermelon?")

He took his large, yellow knife out of his pocket and split that sweet Texas melon in half, handing me a large chunk to take inside for Epis and me to enjoy later. I stood at the front door at 12:20 AM, watching my dad and the *hombres* chow down on juicy, red watermelon. *God brought all these folks together*, I thought.

My father bade me good-bye and said, "Thank you, *mija*," at least three times. Then he called to the hombres, "Let's go, boys! Load up!" He turned back to me. "Hug Epis for me, and tell your man that I came by. Take care of yourself, *mija*. We have to leave now. I hope you understand."

As all the younger *hombres* climbed into the back of the pickup, gentleman Humberto came to say, "*Adios, y gracias!*" I gave him a quick embrace and wished him well.

Humberto continued to work for my dad for six wonderful years and was a very loyal and hardworking hand. I feel in my heart that it was Humberto who hung my daughter's diapers on the line so long ago.

CHAPTER 6:
LOST IN THE ARROYO

Time in the parched West Texas desert had a way of passing almost unnoticeably as one day blended into the next. It wasn't long before my husband was home for a few days.

He was pleased with all the work that Humberto and his boys had done in his absence. He couldn't believe that the *vaquillas ladinas* had been in a pen for weeks. They now appeared tame and were ready to be shipped.

The spring calf crop kept my husband running from one ranch to another. He was in charge of five ranches, complete with five different herds of mama cows to medicate and assist.

One particular day, he was checking on cattle at the Rustler Springs Ranch, and he asked if Epis and I would ride with him just a few miles down the road to the "leech pasture," or the sandijuela pasture, as my husband called it (he claimed to have seen leeches in the springs of this pasture). He needed to assist a cow with birthing difficulties and thought we might like to come along. He promised that as a treat, he would stop at the ponds and shoot our supper, dove and quail. Chicken-fried dove and quail with buttermilk biscuits and white gravy was one of his favorite meals.

When we were crossing the *arroyo de el sacate salado (salt draw)*, I thought I saw a man in the distant brush. He appeared to be spinning in circles. I yelled at my husband to stop, but he said, "What would one man be doing in the arroyo spinning in this heat? He could at least wait 'til it cools down a bit!" He laughed loudly and kept on driving.

He was not taking me seriously, so I began to sob.

"Quit crying. It's probably a deer or a lonesome coyote that you saw!" said my doubting husband.

I begged him once again to stop. "I saw gray hair on his head, like Daddy has," I cried. After this pitiful display of emotion, my husband finally stopped. He backed up the Ford a few feet and went to check on this supposed man in the arroyo.

Moments later, he emerged out of the brushy arroyo guiding an elderly, dark-skinned, gray-haired man who walked with a slight limp. The old man appeared lost and distraught. He was mumbling English words, but I could not understand him. The hot desert sun had robbed the old man of his senses. We offered him a cold drink of water and a burrito, which he did not finish. We allowed him plenty of time to compose himself.

Millie and Epis got out of the truck. Millie the dog went for a short walk in the grassy arroyo, but my daughter was more concerned with the old man. She asked, "*Es Welo?* Is that Grandpa? What is he doing here? *Que hace Welo aqui*, Mama?"

Finally, the old man began to speak in a tired and broken English. The man's name was Jose. He had gotten lost and disoriented after a stop at the U.S. Immigration checkpoint in Van Horn, which was approximately fifty miles from where we lived. He explained that U.S. Immigration officials wanted to arrest him, his two nephews, and his son: "We were driving back from Juarez. We did not expect the immigration checkpoint to be open; sometimes it is not open at night. We do not have legal papers, and my nephew brought some stuff to sell." By "stuff," I knew he meant drugs.

"It was every man for himself at the checkpoint," the man continued. "We all jumped out of the car and ran aimlessly into the darkness. I think *La Migra* caught one or maybe two of the boys, but I just kept on running into the darkness. I never did look back. The morning of the next day, I could not find my sons. I called out to them, but no one answered. I just kept walking." Jose's voice trembled.

My husband and I exchanged a glance of concern before telling Jose where we were going. We told him about the mama cow in misery, and he agreed to help us. "We will take you home to our house later, and you can have supper with us," I said. "We may have time to shoot some birds for supper." He smirked and did not seem too interested in eating a wild bird.

The mama cow, as it turned out, would need to be fed and medicated for a few weeks, so Jose and my husband loaded her and her newborn calf in the trailer, and we all headed for home. My husband always brought along the horse trailer for situations such as this.

On the way home, Jose began to speak to me in fluent English. "I have been living in America for many years. My youngest children were born in America. I am a carpenter and build homes for a living. I build beautiful homes, and I own a home here in America. I have a good job and earn good money—probably more money than you make out here. I just have not been able to get my legal residency. But I don't consider myself a wetback. I have a better home than you," he added.

My husband and I exchanged another glance, although this time, it was of a different kind of concern. Jose seemed to be trying to convince himself that his lifestyle was acceptable and much better than ours. Silently, I agreed with him to a certain degree; he probably did make more American money than we did. But I would not trade our life at the Rustler for anyone else's. I loved who I was, my little family, and our beautiful Rustler Springs. What else was there?

At the twin ponds, my husband stopped to shoot our supper. We waited for him quietly, and soon he had shot enough dove and quail for our supper—along with a duck for good measure.

When we arrived at the house, I took Epis and Millie inside. I changed my daughter's clothes and put her down for a nap. Then I fixed two tall glasses of ice-cold lemonade and took them outside to my husband and Jose.

My husband had already gotten the mama cow and her calf situated and was busy plucking birds for supper. He loved to fry dove, quail, and duck and then serve them with smooth, white peppered gravy and hot buttermilk biscuits. He brought buttermilk from headquarters when he was in the mood for these famous biscuits.

"What is this?" asked Jose in a harsh voice. "I don't like lemon water with sugar. I want some iced tea or a Coke—something like that!" I explained to him that we were out of tea and did not keep Coke or other carbonated drinks. Pink lemonade was all we had, besides well water. "I'll just drink water then," he said with a snarl.

I thought of my mannerly friend Humberto, with his warm smile, his gentle disposition, and his respectful manner. *Why can't more men be like Humberto?* I wondered.

At supper, Jose declined my husband's delicious meal. "Don't you have anything else?" Jose asked with no reservations. I prepared a large helping of leftover meatloaf, sliced garden tomatoes, and beans, and Jose devoured the meal as if it were his last supper! He topped it off with two buttermilk biscuits with honey and a large glass of cold water. I could sense anger building in my husband's heart. How dare Jose turn down such a delicious meal, especially since my husband had gone out of his way to prepare the tasty feast! My husband was giving me the look—the one that says, "Don't coddle these people. Just feed them whatever you have on hand and send them on their way."

At sixty-two, Jose was the oldest hombre I encountered that year. Perhaps his attitude reflected disappointment with his own life. Perhaps walking many miles in three-digit temperatures had taken its toll. Perhaps at this age, he had dreams of living comfortably in his home in America instead of scurrying through the scorching desert. Or perhaps he was disappointed in his family's illegal status, which had temporarily robbed him of his freedom (and, apparently, his proud social standing). Jose's nephew had added to his grief by bringing drugs into the country and arousing suspicion.

I felt sorry for him. He had a lot of the same features as my daddy. He was, after all, somebody's grandpa!

Some of Jose's family members lived in a nearby town. My husband contacted them by phone from Orla, and they quickly came and took Jose home. Years later, I ran into Jose in town. He had mellowed somewhat. I did not ask him any questions for fear of embarrassing him; I just shook his hand, gave him a hug, and wished him well.

After our experience with Jose, my husband and I settled into our regular ranch routine. Outside, I could feel the last days of summer approaching. The days were longer and hotter, and the *hombres* just kept coming. They were a tenacious people who did not give up easily. I tried hard to understand them and even harder not to judge them. I knew that in the Bible, Jesus said to feed the poor, so I wanted to feed all of them. I knew that society would judge me for helping illegal immigrants, but at the time, I could not worry about other people's opinions. Helping these people was the least I could do; after all, they were human, just like me. I could see some of me in all of them. I only did for them what I hoped someone would do for me if I were ever in the same situation.

CHAPTER 7:
THE SANDSTORM STRANGER

In March of 1974, the West Texas wind blew mercilessly across the hills and plains. Some days the dust and sand were so thick that one could not see more than a few inches beyond the swirl of soil. Small slivers of wood and tiny pebbles armed the windstorms with shrapnel. Sometimes the sandstorms would last for one day; sometimes they would last much longer, creating misery upon the land for animal and man alike. On days like these, I would open the barn door for Cinnamon and Barker (my watchdogs), so they could seek shelter from the harsh, wild whipping of the desert winds. In just a few minutes, the wind could destroy a flourishing vegetable garden, leaving only tattered leaves and broken vines; winds also scattered most of the feathered community living high in the cottonwood trees, salt cedars, and silver leaf poplars.

On one particular day, the wind was howling furiously, blowing red sand and dust, when I heard Cinnamon barking in the distance. I looked out my window but could only see blowing dust and sand. Then I thought I heard both Barker and Cinnamon barking, so I opened the front door and stuck my head out, shielding my eyes with my hands. There, cowering by the old tire barn, I could distinguish the silhouette of a man daring the windstorm.

I yelled, "Hey, come here! Hey, over here! Come here!" The silhouette wasn't moving. It stood stoic, like an Egyptian statue in the sand. As I watched, the silhouette began to move so slowly that he appeared to be standing still, facing the opposite direction from me, with his hands over his face. I decided to call to him in Spanish: "*Senor, venga aqui! Venga pronto!*" The tall, shadowlike figure walked backward toward me with Barker and Cinnamon escorting him along, struggling against the howling wind and blasting sand. My dogs yearned for company, so they weren't about to attack him; instead, they led the way. They now appeared comfortable with this sandstorm stranger who had come to visit.

The sandstorm would not let up for hours. From the doorway, I invited our guest in for a much needed drink of water and a bite to eat. In through the front door of the Rustler bunkhouse walked the most pitiful, skinny, and pale middle-aged man. Sunken red eyes peered at me from under a thick, dusty brow. He sported an old, worn cowboy hat that had done what it could to shield him from the vicious storm; it was secured on his head with a piece of string. He stood there quietly, not saying one word.

I said, "*Sientese, por favor.* Please, sit down. *Agua, café?*" I set a cold glass of water and a hot cup of coffee in front of him simultaneously.

He sat there for a few moments, sipped his water slowly, and finally said, "*Se nos acabo la comida hace unos dias y la noche de la tormenta nos separamos en las montanas. No puedo hallar los otros companeros. Se nos acabo tambien el agua.*" Before I could respond, he continued to explain, with a level of fear in his voice, "*Llovio mucho; muchos truenos; nos separamos; tengo miedo enfermarme si tomo mucha agua o si como comida, y ahora con esta tormenta de arena.*"

The trembling fear in the voice of this mature man almost made me cry. He had been traveling with several other people, but they were separated during a ferocious thunderstorm in the mountains.

"I looked for them," he continued, speaking in a wavering Spanish voice. "I could not find them. We were out of water and food. I am afraid to drink water or to eat food now, because it might make me sick to my stomach. It rained a lot. There was a lot of thunder. I don't know where the others are." I stood there listening, safe in my cozy kitchen, wondering how many other souls might be in the mountains, lost in the storm of continuous poverty and despair. My daughter awoke from her afternoon nap; the tiny tot stood by my side and stared at the dusty stranger. I think she had questions of her own.

The stranger in our house did not talk much after explaining his current situation. He sat and absorbed his surroundings for what seemed like a long time. Then he stood, thanked me politely, and said, "I would like to rest before I eat; I don't want to get sick. Why don't you wrap that food for me? I will eat it later. I will take more water. I need a larger container for water."

Without delay, I searched the cabinet under the kitchen sink and handed him a large plastic container. He filled it with fresh water, appearing pleased with the large container. I pointed to the door of the red hay barn where he could go and rest.

By the next morning, the windstorm had diminished. I stepped out and called our most recent guest in for a hearty ranch breakfast, but no reply came. Our guest had disappeared overnight along with the whirling West Texas winds.

I never saw or heard from him again. I never got his name or the rest of his story. I still wonder if he ever crossed paths with his companeros again; I still wonder who he was and what his destination was. One thing I am sure of is that American money played a role in his decision to walk to America—directly into a roaring devil of dust.

CHAPTER 8:
SHARING SANDIA AT CAVE RANCH

The late summer of 1974 brought sweet watermelon, honeydew melons, and Pecos cantaloupes to our dinner table.

One hot day, my husband and I decided to go check on a friend whom we had not heard from for over three months. We wanted to make sure that he was doing well and offer some of our sweet melons to him. I packed a large picnic lunch and included most of the sweet, ripe melons. My husband, meanwhile, prepared the old water can with fresh ice water and a large jug of tea.

As we drove down the rough ranch roads with our daughter in tow, I noticed that the road did not appear to have been traveled recently. I looked for these sorts of things while doing my so-called studies in the field. The road showed no recent tire tracks, and the dryness of the pastures added concern to what I was already feeling. We did encounter a few very poor, scrawny cows. Life seemed to have forgotten the Cave Ranch. I did not see but a few wildflowers along the way. The dust and dry heat added misery to what had started out to be another grand day at Rustler Springs.

Unconcerned, my husband shrugged off my observations.

"There must be another entry road to the Cave Ranch," he said.

I recalled how the eight men had appeared in our horse corrals just months before. *Are we going to find the same situation at the Cave Ranch?*

When we stopped to open the gate that leads to the Cave Ranch house, we saw three men quickly approaching us. We were still about a mile from the house, but the roar of the old blue Ford motor had brought them running, desperately seeking help.

When they approached the gate, my husband's friend started to yell: "*Necesitamos ayuda! Ayudenos por favor! Tenemos mucho hambre!*" ("We need help! Please help us! We are very hungry!")

My silent suspicions had come true: we had another case of starving human beings.

"But why are they starving?" I asked my bewildered husband. He just could not accept the fact that some American employers could treat their hired help in this way; he always looked for the best in everyone.

My husband said to his muy flaco amigo, "Quizas a tus patrones se les olvido que ustedes estaban aqui." ("Maybe your employers forgot that you are here.")

"How can they forget the hired help for three months and not forget the number of cattle they have on the Cave Ranch?" I said to my husband in an angry voice. "Most ranchers can tell you exactly how many mother cows and how many bulls they have! Yet, these folks forgot that they have hired hands looking after their cattle." When I saw the concerned look on my husband's face, I decided to be quiet and help. I did not want my daughter to see people in this ungodly condition again, but we both had to endure and help my husband feed these three ravenous souls.

I unpacked the picnic basket and set out the food on the tailgate of the blue Ford.

Lupe, my husband's friend, advised us that they had well water to drink but had not had food for a while. They had been living on birds, jackrabbits, lizards, and rats that they killed with stones. Without hesitation, they dove into the buffet set before them, and they ate, ate, and ate.

After dinner, the workers continued to tell their story of life at the Cave Ranch. There had been six workers at first, they said, but the other three *hombres* had left a few days before; they were tired of battling the heat, the scorpions, the hunger, and their heartless boss. "They walked back to Mexico without pay," said Lupe.

They all sat on the porch and drank cool water from the large aluminum water can. It was a pleasant change from the water in their man-made well, which usually had critters floating in it.

As my daughter and her pup napped on a cot on the rotting wooden porch, my husband unloaded the box of fragrant melons from the back of the pickup. The three *hombres* snatched the box from my husband's hands. Even after each had selected a melon, they coveted each other's melons! Their miserable hunger prompted their fear of running out of food once again.

What happened next surprised even my husband: the men hid the food that was left after their all-you-can-eat buffet. They hid their melons in different parts of the aging ranch house. They ate only from the sweet melon that we had cut and stored in a large plastic container. Severe hunger had caused these men to store and hoard food, much like the rodents they had been eating for weeks.

The next day, my husband stopped by the Cave Ranch headquarters and kindly reminded the folks there of their starving employees. Just a few days after that, we learned that Lupe and his two malnourished friends had been arrested and deported by the U.S. Border Patrol. 1974 was not a good year for Lupe and friends.

CHAPTER 9:
A FAMILY OF THREE

Autumn was in the air. The roar and rumble of the distant geophysical seismograph crews rolled across the northern pasture. These crews often came by the ranch for fresh cistern water and a visit; today would be one of those days.

A crew of four men drove up under the trees and helped themselves to fresh water. One man was walking toward our house, so I went outside to see what he wanted. "Did those people come by for food and water?" he asked, pointing northeast from where we were standing. "See them over there in the draw? We stopped to talk to them and offered them water, but they just kept on walking. There is a man, a woman, and a girl not more than ten years old." His concern was apparent in his voice. "There they are—do you see them?" I could see what appeared to be humans walking east at a fast pace, but I could not distinguish if they were male or female.

"Why would they just walk by without stopping for food and water?" I asked. "I would have given them assistance and a place to rest." We stood there, staring in their direction until they were out of sight. I did not have a vehicle, or I would have gone to check on them. I was concerned about the young girl walking such a long distance. What would possess parents to bring a child on such a dreadful trip? The seismograph crew also expressed concern for the child, but their offers to help had been declined. The fear of being caught and deported along with their young daughter had probably persuaded the determined parents to keep on walking.

The low spots of the Rio Bravo and the lust for American money continued to entice the desperate and the forlorn. They fled deplorable living conditions in Mexico and other Third World countries for a better life in America.

Unfortunately, little did they know that they could experience deplorable living conditions right here in America, too. Justo, the frail man from the Twin Caves Ranch who had been forced to sleep on the rotting wooden floor without a bed or blanket, had been promised money, food, and supplies in exchange for general labor. Yet, when he had come over to our place seeking help, he had been surviving on black coffee and stewed tomatoes for days.

The old Twin Caves Ranch House had not offered good living conditions to anyone for many years. My own family had lived there many years before. My brothers and I had found it amusing that there were bats inside the house. The bats lived in the old fireplace and came out at night to play my brothers' own version of baseball. The bats themselves were the baseballs; long sticks served as baseball bats for my three mischievous brothers.

The large, wooden house was overrun by desert packrats, mice, roaches, Mexican free-tailed bats, spiders, red ants, fleas, ticks, biting flies, and—worst of all—hungry black and red bloodsucking beetles.

No dog or cat could have survived there without being bit or catching a disease, yet human beings were expected to live and work there. This is the part of the illegal immigrants' so-called American dream that we don't hear enough about.

As the family of three disappeared over the horizon, I felt emptiness in my heart and I silently wished happy trails to all of them, especially to their young daughter.

Chapter 10:
Little Green Men

During the winter, I rarely heard from anyone except my immediate family. They lived in Toyah, approximately fifty-four miles south of the Rustler. Two brothers, three sisters, and my mother lived there at the time. They came to visit at both Thanksgiving and Christmas that year. Venison, diced canned tomatoes and onion bake (or Rustler steak as we called it) was on the menu for the Christmas holiday, along with tender baked quail and cornbread dressing.

My family also brought ham and sweet potatoes.

Months went by without little incident; then came summer vacation for one of my sisters. Out of school and bored, she begged our mother to let her stay with me for a week. My husband thought it was a good idea. "Her company will be good for you," he said. "It's about time you had company." I was thrilled for her to stay.

Both my husband and my family left the Rustler in the early evening hours. My family went back to Toyah, and my husband went back to headquarters to keep an eye out for trespassers during the Fourth of July holiday. I guess he just assumed that we would be alright, alone at the Rustler. My family and husband happily bid us a happy Independence Day and drove off in different directions.

Late that night, my sister and I told stories about aliens from outer space and flying saucers as we dined on hot coffee with milk and *gaznates*, a type of Mexican sweetbread.

Six *hombres* lived at a neighboring ranch about fifteen miles away. These *hombres* had access to a vehicle and often went to town to buy liquor. I had heard their stories from my husband. The Fourth of July offered just another reason for them to go to Pecos and buy liquor. They had been drinking for some time when they decided to pay me a visit.

Apparently, they had felt fairly sure that I would be alone, so they waited until nightfall, loaded themselves up with a generous helping of gall, and came on over. I had just gotten up from my rocking chair to put on a fresh pot of coffee when, in the distance, I noticed little red lights in the brush of the west draw. I knew that this was no flying saucer! It could only be the persistent *gringo* in the red and white truck or some other idiot out to cause dismay. Whoever it was, they had parked in the brushy west draw to avoid detection. However, the parking lights had been left on by my insecure suitors.

This can only mean trouble, I thought. *Where is Humberto when I need him? Why me and why now?*

I feared sexual assault, torture, and death for all three of us. But I was not about to go down without one hell of a fight! After all, I had two shotguns, a .30-30 deer rifle, and a .22-caliber rifle at my disposal. I did not really care what my suitors had; I was sure that they did not have firearms.

I immediately advised my young sister to take Epis and Millie to my bedroom and to stay there with them.

Meanwhile, I checked the locks on the back door and turned off our two oil lamps. I explained the importance of being quiet to the girls. They were already weeping silently, so I allowed them to follow me to the front room and get on the bed by the back door. I also showed my sister where the second shotgun was. "If you have to, just aim and shoot," I instructed the shivering youngster. As I prepared my stand by the side window facing the west draw, I noticed that the life inside of me felt stiff and stressed. I gave my extended belly a reassuring massage and then focused on the safety of my girls and the problem at hand.

The moon over the western desert worked in my favor, lighting up the night like a flaming floodlight; I could see everything far and wide. So could my sister, who sobbed uncontrollably. "I see men walking around outside!" she cried. Suddenly, I heard whispering voices and could see men scattering in the dark.

I stood there on trembling knees, also in the dark but on the opposite side of the wall. My shaky hands tightened on my weapon as I quickly concocted my own plan of attack.

Suddenly, I heard a loud sound at the front door, so I aimed my double-barreled shotgun at the door and yelled, "What do you want?"

My lips and hand trembled as I waited for a response.

The indignant masculine voice on the other side of the door said in Spanish, "Oh ... pret ... ty ... we come to talk with you. Open the door! We know that your man is not here, because his blue truck is not here."

"I do not want to talk to you. You must leave this place or suffer the consequences of your actions," I said gallantly. Just then, my sister let out a shrieking cry.

My suitors now realized that I was not alone, and the one at the door said, "Uh-oh. Who is in there with you? I hear a little girl. Who is she? Is she pretty like you?" *Death*, I thought. *We are face to face with sure death!*

My thoughts were interrupted by a loud, impatient voice growling, "Answer me, *bonita*, or I will knock down the damn door!"

With my beating heart in my throat, I repeated, "*Tienen que irse de aqui o sufrir las consequencias!*" ("You must leave this place or suffer the consequences!") My sister's wailing was distracting me, so I instructed her to go back to the bed with Epis.

I reminded her of the other shotgun and reassured her that it was easy to shoot. "Just point in the direction of the intruders and shoot. You can't miss! You can do it! Now be brave, and go on!"

Just then, the man at the front door turned the knob, pushing on the door. So I shifted gears, built up a quick helping of my own damn gall, and yelled, "*Oyeme!* Listen to me!" Then I let him hear me cock the shotgun. The click of the shotgun brought silence from the other side of the door.

"If you touch the door one more time," I yelled in a trembling and frightened voice, "your *amigos* will have to pick you up in small bloody pieces from the ground. There is a double-barreled shotgun waiting for you!" I put the .22 rifle behind a curtain, but within reach, as I continued to aim at the door with my trusty double-barrel shotgun.

The sudden quiet in the night was almost unbearable; even my sister quit crying. Time stood still as we waited for his response.

"There are six of us and only two of you," said the man at the door in a threatening, macho voice.

By now, my Mexican blood was boiling! "There will be only five of you left, you idiot, because you will be painted across the earth," I said. "And if I have to, I will take out one more of you. I will take out whoever is standing by the west window." The dark silhouette at the west window slowly slid down to the ground. I could still see the form of his cowardly head from where I was standing.

Once again, silence filled the air. My apprehensive heart fixed itself in my throat, threatening to choke me. I wanted to vomit. I didn't want to resort to violence, but I feared for my girls and their safety. *Even Millie the dog is in danger with this bunch*, I thought. *They will kill us all!*

Then I heard the slam of the front screen door, and my stalker yell in a loud, disappointed voice, "You damn wild woman! You probably would shoot me, wouldn't you?" With that, he called to his *amigos*, and they all made a quick retreat to their partially hidden truck, cursing and yelling obscenities.

My sister sighed in relief as she rushed to give me a hug. "You did it, Lou! You did it! They're gone! I can't believe how you handled the man at the door. I could hear him breathing; he was so close. You made a believer out of him! You did it!" Tears welled in her eyes. I just stood there, nauseated, holding her tightly.

I never did let my guard down that night; I feared that the real-life version of aliens might return in the wee hours of the morning. So I put my sister to bed with Epis and Millie and then remained vigilant until early the next day. I couldn't let my sister know the fear I felt inside. It was a burning, paralyzing fear that turned my stomach for the rest of the night. I wanted her to be a strong, young woman—stronger than me—who could defend herself in a situation such as this.

While I sat there in the dark, pondering and reflecting in the comfort of my rocking chair, I realized that the phrase "little green men" now had a whole new meaning. Considering their cowardice, the new phrase should be "little yellow men!" After midnight and after a good cry, I fixed myself a fresh cup of coffee.

When my husband returned the next evening, my sister and I told him about our frightening ordeal with our Independence Day suitors. He got in his truck, drove to the Brooks Ranch, and spoke with the supervisor. Two days later, the six *hombres* were deported by the U.S. Border Patrol. Nothing else was ever said about our dangerous and unfortunate dilemma.

CHAPTER 11:
HOT COFFEE WITH LARD

Most of the people I met in 1973 and 1974 were poor peasant farmers suffering a real monetary need. They were vulnerable to abuse by American employers looking for cheap labor.

As the brisk winds of late autumn escorted leaves to the ground, the influx of illegal immigrants started to flow again like the muddy waters of the Rio Grande that they were determined to cross.

My husband's work ritual continued as he rotated from one ranch to another. On this particular day, however, he planned to drive to a neighboring ranch and return the same evening. I saw an opportunity to tag along. After a few minutes of discussion, he allowed my daughter and I to go with him. We were so excited! We had not been anywhere for months, so this was a treat for us.

"We can come back through Toyah, so you can visit with your family for a bit," he said.

Coming back through Toyah would make this a long trip—approximately one hundred miles. My pregnancy would make the distance seem even longer. With my delivery due date just weeks away, I had to go to the bathroom often. Trying to find a bathroom along a dusty dirt road was not easy. Squatting behind a bush might sound easy, but my giant, protruding belly made it almost impossible.

On the bumpy road to Toyah, I just could not hold it any longer; my poor, swollen bladder was aching. I was to the point of crying, so I persuaded my unwilling husband to pull in at a ranch that appeared abandoned. "You are not going to find a bathroom here!" he snapped.

"Please, stop the truck and let me do my business," I begged.

I quickly explained to him that I was not looking for a proper bathroom, just a place that offered plenty of room and privacy away from the main road. "I might fall over while trying to squat—or, worse yet, I might pee all over myself! I may need to change clothes! I need room … lots of room!" I cried.

My initially uncooperative husband finally came to a stop under a large shade tree in the yard of the old abandoned ranch house, by an old wet shack.

I got off the truck with his assistance and stumbled around until I couldn't hold it any longer—I just pulled my pants down and began to pee. My husband held half of me up with one hand while he smoked a cigarette with the other. I held my other half up by leaning on the truck. I was adjusting my position when I looked up to see a depressingly thin man standing by the wet shack.

"Look!" I yelled. "There is a man leaning on the corner of that shack!"

"You don't waste any time, do you?" my husband grumbled. "You're always seeing things!"

As my husband continued to mutter, and as I fought with my clothes to pull them back up, the thin man stepped out of the shadows and began to speak.

"*Buenas tardes. Tengo mucho hambre. No traen comida?*" the man whispered, his voice apparently weakened by hunger. ("Good evening. I am very hungry. Do you have food?")

We could only offer him vanilla wafers that we had packed for Epis on this long trip. I was horrified to hear his story—and to see his ribs aligning the sides of his tattered shirt. He had been hired on at this ranch as a ranch hand and had been supplied with some food initially. He had been promised money and more food if he remained there and took care of the place. For some unknown reason, his employers had never returned. He did not know what day of the week it was or how long he had been waiting. He only knew that he had been without food for many, many days. He was surviving on hot coffee and one large tablespoon of lard per day. Piping hot coffee and pork lard—that was all this man had to eat.

I was appalled at the people who had hired him. We quickly offered him our box of vanilla wafers before leaving for Toyah. "We will return with food," we assured him.

At Toyah, I gathered my family together and informed them of this poor man's situation. Not surprisingly, they all pitched in with food, aspirin, and enough money for him to buy a bus ticket should he decide to go home. My husband and my eldest brother, Julian, delivered the goods to this starving soul that same night.

The next day, my eldest brother and my husband took the man to the bus stop, where he bought a one way ticket to El Paso, Texas. I had witnessed horror stories like his before, but it never got easier. Such one-on-one experiences broke my heart and put everything into a different perspective. I made all kinds of judgments and conclusions about my fellow man, and I did not like what I was feeling. I was somewhat confused.

We arrived at the Rustler after midnight. I was exhausted from the trip with my husband. *Never again*, I thought. *I will never again ask my hardworking husband to let me tag along. He has my blessing to go and work wherever and whenever he wants.*

I would be glad to stay behind in my comfortable little bunkhouse and listen to the rustling songs of the leaves high above the cool, meandering waters of the springs.

The next day, before my husband left to check in at headquarters, four more *hombres* came pacing through, looking for food, water, and a place to rest. I now knew the routine like the back of my hand.

CHAPTER 12:
PACKRATS FOR LUNCH

Again and again, the state of Chihuahua, Mexico, sent me its weak and forsaken. These latest four were in a pitiful state.

Three of them had been to America before; one man was here for the first time. The stress lines on his face made him appear older than the other three. He had been sick to his stomach for several days and had a bony outline to prove it. He introduced himself as Pascual.

I explained to the sick hombre that the pain in his stomach might be hunger, so I offered him a taquito.

He replied in a nauseated voice, "Oh, no! It was a taquito that caused the misery in my belly—a taquito of medium rare roasted packrat!"

His *companeros* quickly explained that after running out of food in the desert, they had resorted to digging packrats out of their dens and roasting them over an open fire. Pascual and his friends had dined on roasted packrat for two days before arriving at the Rustler. "We also killed a skunk, but he was too stinky to eat," said Pascual.

As the men sat down under the shade of knotted cedars by the spring, I scurried off to the kitchen to cook a quick meal. Steamed *fideos* and refried beans (my old favorites) simmered slowly as I made a fresh batch of homemade flour tortillas on a hot comal.

"Feed them and send them on their way," directed my husband as he walked out the door.

"Y'all come and eat," I yelled.

The pleasant smell of simmering, fresh beans brought all four *hombres* to the dinner table.

Pascual ate only a few bites and then stepped outside with a stomach ache. His three companions ate all the *fideos* and most of the refried beans, which were flavored with bacon fat. The pile of soft, warm flour tortillas disappeared in the company of peanut butter and honey.

Like all of their brothers before them, the four *hombres* spent one night in the hay barn and left before daylight the next day. Armed with bean burritos and fresh water, they trampled off on their own quest in the land of milk and money.

My last year back at the Rustler proved to be a test of tolerance, patience, love for my fellow man, and enduring faith. The determination of these people forced me to take a good hard look at myself.

I, a young American, could never have walked the rocky, thorny, and dusty trails that these illegal immigrants walked. I would never risk my life enduring the elements just to earn less than minimum wage. I felt slightly ashamed of my physical capabilities—but proud and extremely fortunate to be an American. Maybe my parents were not so ignorant after all.

Chapter 13:
Desert Feline Soup

My simple American lifestyle seemed like that of a princess in her castle compared to the meager lifestyle of the wandering and unwavering illegal immigrants. I will always be thankful to God for his generosity, his love, and his patience.

The worst story I heard that year was gross enough to give an avid hill person like myself a strong bout of nausea and a sour stomach.

Two years earlier, autumn leaves were falling when three hombres from the state of Chihuahua had decided unanimously that it was once again time to cross the Rio Grande illegally into America. More American money was needed to sustain their farm plots in Mexico, which yielded a yearly supply of beans, corn, and hot peppers. This vegetable crop was their major source of income in Mexico, but they felt that another trip to America was inevitable. They planned to return to their beloved Chihuahua in late summer with enough American money to support them for another year.

Determined, the three *hombres* traveled by bus from Chihuahua City to Ojinaga, Mexico, across the border from Presidio, Texas. There they spent a couple of days in a run-down motel, plotting and planning their trip to America. On the evening of the third day, they walked to the outskirts of Ojinaga and sought a safe place to cross the Rio Bravo (Rio Grande), away from the peering binoculars of the U.S. Border Patrol.

The three daring illegals then trekked the Sierra Vieja mountain range, braved the treacherous Chihuahuan desert, and taunted the blistering sun on their quest for American money. They headed northwest with the Dilihunt Ranch as their final destination. In their backpacks they carried flour tortillas, a bag of pinole (a type of corn mush, usually seasoned with cinnamon sugar), and jugs of water.

One meticulous man also carried a large, empty aluminum can to use as a cook pot, along with salt, pepper, and garlic cloves wrapped in tinfoil, should the need arise. The homemade pot would prove to be a lifesaver for the adventurous trio.

Three days later, their expedition proved to be a harsh one as they found themselves hot, exhausted, and deep in the western Chihuahuan desert without any water or food. They tried hard to recall the location of windmills and livestock dirt tanks along the path to a better life, but the blistering sun and the elements deprived the three of their geographical senses.

They finally arrived at a windmill with a large, tall, steel holding tank. As they approached the tank to get a much-needed drink of water, they noticed an unfortunate bobcat floating in the water. The water level in the tank was low, and the bobcat had apparently leaned in to get a drink of water, fallen, and drowned.

They rushed quickly to get the cat out of the tank and noticed that its body was only slightly bloated; this could mean that the cat had not been in the water very long. The three hungry *hombres* drank windmill water to their satisfaction, and then they focused on the drowned bobcat carcass. After a short discussion, their hunger dilemma was settled: they would feast on desert feline soup that very night!

They quickly dressed out the soaking-wet cat. They prepared the large tin can with boiling water for *caldito de gato montes*.

Large strips of prime cat tenders were cut, rinsed, and tossed into the boiling water. These cuts were seasoned with salt, pepper, and garlic from the tinfoil. They hung the leathery, tan and white bobcat skin on the fence as a sign of their good fortune.

The *hombres* had little reservations about eating drowned bobcat. This was their only source of food at the time, and they were determined to live to earn American money.

Empty stomachs rumbled with anticipation as the smell of boiled desert feline filled the air around the windmill. The three eager *hombres* took a short rest by the shade of the tall steel tank. They discussed their good fortune of finding food and water concurrently. Dropping to their bony knees, they gratefully said, "*Gracias a Dios!*" ("Thanks be to God!")

Hours later, the three men sat around the small, mesquite-fueled fire and dined on tender chunks of boiled Texas bobcat seasoned to a turn from their tinfoil cache.

"Desert feline soup is rich and delicious," said one of the fortunate three. The misfortune of a thirsty desert bobcat had become the fortune of three famished lives.

Two years later, sitting under a shade tree at the Rustler Springs Ranch, the man who had dressed out the bobcat, boiled it in the homemade cooking pot, and who had gratifyingly eaten it told his story. He informed me that the "bobcat boil," similar to shrimp boil, did not taste bad at all. "The drowned bobcat meat was sweet and tender, and was not stringy or leathery at all," said the fortunate man.

The man telling the bobcat-boil story eventually became my husband of nineteen years. He was an illegal immigrant working for a generous West Texas rancher when I met him in 1972. I met him at the Rustler Springs ranch, on one of my many visits back to the home where I was raised.

I had always been intrigued by the lifestyle of these hardworking people, so I married one and thereby gained experience in the field, as I often joked. The subject of my field experiment was six foot three, weighed 175 pounds, and was the hardest working cowboy I had ever seen. He was well dressed, well liked, and respected by his employers. He was a dedicated employee who always put his job first. He was a good husband and father.

We remained married for nineteen years and are parents to three lovely and very independent children.

He is now a resident alien because of me and is able to work anywhere in America if he so chooses. Now in his seventies, he still manages to work a job outside the home, in spite of some physical limitations.

CHAPTER 14:
ILLEGAL IMMIGRATION

TODAY

Illegal immigration has been a thorn in America's side for hundreds of years. Today, illegal immigration is out of control. The time has come for serious and more humane immigration reform.

The current Bureau of U.S. Immigration and Customs Enforcement has done a great job, given the rising number of illegal immigrants who cross our borders daily. I praise its ongoing efforts. But the huge influx of illegal immigrants coupled with homeland security issues and the illegal drug trade call for a strict new immigration reform system. As described in the Immigration section of Change.gov (http://change.gov/agenda/ immigration_agenda, henceforth "Change.gov"), the site used by President Obama to transition into his administration, the new reform system must be willing to enforce all existing laws and possibly impose stiff fines on all American employers who hire illegal immigrants. Imposing higher taxes for these employers might also discourage them from hiring illegal immigrants. The new Immigration Reform system must model discipline through education.

As noted in the Fact Sheets section of the Web site of U.S. Immigration and Customs Enforcement (www.ice.gov/pi/news/factsheets), the current system does imprison and deport illegal immigrants, but it lacks more direct federal oversight. Additional management staff is needed to address the large percentage of complaints about the current immigration detention system (discipline through education). The ideal immigration detention system would include self-discipline, education, and training. We must not forget that American employers seeking cheap labor make up one half of the illegal-immigration pie. The other half of the pie is made up by the incoming illegal immigrant masses that cross U.S. borders on a daily basis to provide that cheap labor.

One option worth considering is that of offering citizenship to young illegal immigrants living peacefully within the United States in exchange for their active duty and participation (at least two years) in the U.S. military. Also worth considering is the furthering of the education, via GED classes (and beyond if the grades are there) or job training, of any person willing to enter this country legally, to obey American laws, and to become an American citizen. This idea could enhance immigrant lives by offering higher expectations for subsequent generations while assuring America of a less dependent population and a more secure future.

TOMORROW

Any new immigration reform bill should include a more creative and disciplined approach to illegal immigration. The idea of a million-dollar border fence includes neither. In just a short time, many illegal immigrants have mastered the hop over the towering fence.

I understand and agree that we must take drastic measures to secure our borders from terrorists, drug dealers, and the thousands of illegal immigrants who just want to make America their home. But let's face facts: As long as there are millions of American dollars to be made from the illegal drug trade, from the illegal gun trade, and from American employers seeking cheap labor, the drug dealers, terrorists, and masses will continue to come. Those who commit illegal acts are ready to meet whatever obstacles, including a tall costly fence, that stands between them and American money. Yet we, the Americans, don't pose many obstacles on the course of tomorrow's illegal immigrant.

America doesn't pose an obstacle with its overworked and possibly underpaid U.S. Border Patrol Service that is distributed far too thinly across the enormous area that they are expected to patrol. This shortcoming must be dealt with swiftly by increasing the manpower on the border, along with their hourly/monthly wages. America could recruit young immigrants caught crossing the border illegally and offer them the opportunity to train under special U.S. forces, serving as border guards on either side of the border, in exchange for shortened or no prison time in America. Thus, many could earn American money while still remaining in their homeland. The Mexican border guards would be subject to all American rules, laws, and expectations.

Some formal education and special training could open new doors for all those who are willing to enter legally and for all those who are willing to enrich our homeland security programs with their knowledge and skills.

Our current American society isn't discouraging illegal immigrants, but baiting them. Thousands of employers are willing to hire illegal immigrants in order to save a few of those coveted American dollars. With all due respect and admiration for our great country, I feel that I must make this point.

As long as many Americans continue using illegal drugs and using illegal aliens as cheap labor, immigrants from all over the world will flock to America, much like the great caribou herds of the north that look for green during the cold season. Illegal immigrants will learn to pole vault, dig tunnels like moles, and otherwise find their way over, under, around, and through the very expensive and intrusive U.S. border fence and the border it is supposed to protect. The fence creates border calamity and distrust among two allied countries, which together should be focused on abating the illegal migrations to the north.

Mexico could provide some manpower from the south side of the fence, and America could provide American money from the north, which would enrich our current Homeland Security Program and lifestyles for all. Both countries could benefit from a program such as this.

The fence now affects the lifestyles and traditions of many families that have been living along both sides of the river for many years. It also affects the ecosystem of the Rio Grande as we know it, changing the ambience of river property, therefore affecting its value. The fence denies the property rights of some Texas ranchers, universities, parks, and so on.

The Rio Grande will continue to flow, and so will the steady stream of illegal immigrants seeking the promised land of milk and money. Any new U.S. immigration law or reform would benefit from high expectations from all Americans and all future Americans.

Any new immigration system could benefit from a discipline method that I learned during my first year of teaching at a large and wonderful district in West Texas. The school district was teaching and practicing the five "R" disciplinary problem-solving method, which encouraged students to analyze a problem in a group setting and decide on a solution that meets the five "R" standards. My revised five "R" method, offered in more detail in the next section, calls for a solution to illegal immigration that is reasonable, respectable, reliable, responsible, and rational. Unfortunately, the border fence as an illegal-immigration solution falls under another "R": ridiculous.

Because we must remain positive concerning any new immigration reform, illegal immigrant education along the border fence would be a good issue to dissect during the new U.S. Immigration reform mission in 2010. After all, education will ease the management of any new immigration reform system, and discipline will have to be practiced by all and taught to all— especially to all who continue to enter our country illegally and to all those who continue to hire them. Penalties for repeat offenders on either side must not be lenient. They must be strictly enforced, and repeat offenders must be educated on the benefits of entering the country legally.

All illegal immigrants who have been residing in America for more than 5 years should be held accountable for three mandatory requirements in order to remain in America (in a process also described on White House.gov):

1. Pay a decent fine calculated according to the number of years the illegal immigrant has lived in America;

2. Take a citizenship test and become a U.S. citizen;

3. Pass a high-school equivalency test.

Anyone who fails any of these tests the first time could be given three opportunities to pass in a one year period or face deportation. All parties involved would have to display self-discipline. If any new immigration reform program is to succeed, finger-pointing and blaming must be removed from the discussion table.

My Simple Proposal on U.S. Immigration Reform

During my first four years of teaching in West Texas, I learned about the five "R" disciplinary method for at-risk students. After much research on illegal immigration, I concluded that the five "R" disciplinary method could apply to illegal immigration as well.

The Five "R" Immigration Reform Program

- Reasonable Immigration Reform
- Respectable Immigration Reform
- Reliable Immigration Reform
- Responsible Immigration Reform
- Rational Immigration Reform

*The Reasonable Principle of the Five "R" Immigration Reform Program would include improved efforts to control the human influx on our borders by collaborating with countries whose nationals are willing to participate in our new program—one based on education. Immigrants must be willing to enter our country legally. This new education-based program must be the stronghold for ongoing efforts to enrich homeland security and decrease illegal immigration.

The new immigration reform program would offer informative literature on legal entry to anyone caught entering this country illegally. The right program would provide American employers with much-needed employees (via temporary work visas) when no American workers are willing to do the job. Let's face facts: Most undocumented workers are experts of labor. They display admirable tenacity and unlimited resourcefulness (like Humberto, for example). They are hardworking people willing to accept jobs and wages that many Americans would not ever consider. The employers, jobs, and wages would have to be closely monitored by the U.S. government to avoid any social exploitation of immigrants.

The new immigration reform program would also include a reasonable amount of education as an incentive for those people willing to enter our country legally; willing to respect and obey our current laws; and willing to become American citizens.

*The Respectable Principle of the Five "R" Immigration Reform Program would include and promote compassion. The program would issue temporary work visas to those undocumented workers who are already working here (and who lack a criminal record) as well as to those willing to come over, work, and return home the next day, week, or month. Participants would have to be carefully screened and allowed to travel back and forth between our two countries without fear of being denied their work permits.

The work permits of these temporary employees would be renewed annually or biannually; this renewal would include a new background screening. Any worker convicted of committing crimes in America or in their home country while working under this program would be denied re-entry, thus denying them the opportunity to earn American money. The temporary work program would have to be in accordance with accepted standards of correctness and human decency.

The Respectable Principle would also decrease dysfunction in the current immigration bureaucracy and increase the number of legal immigrants by keeping families together and by meeting the demand for jobs that U.S. employers cannot fill.

*The Reliable Principle of the Five "R" Immigration Reform Program denotes the reform program's trustworthiness to deliver on its promises. As noted on the aforementioned White House. gov site, President Obama made progress toward fulfilling the Reliable Principle by signing the Children's Health Insurance Program Reauthorization Act, which provides quality care to some eleven million legal immigrant children and removes any barriers that could prevent legal immigrant children from being covered.

The Reliable Principle would also encourage employers to make a reasonable effort to offer American workers first priority in filling any job vacancy. Employers who continue to break U.S. immigration law by hiring illegal workers would be closely monitored, fined, and punished.

Any illegal workers who do not desire to obey American laws, participate in America's homeland security programs, and take the oath of citizenship would be provided with self-education literature on legal entry before being deported. People must understand through education and discipline that every illegal action has a consequence—and that obedience of the law has its rewards. Those who desire to take the oath of citizenship will be obligated to learn, as they do now (through improved education programs) the facts and policies of American law.

*The Responsible Principle of the Five "R" Immigration Reform Program would require the immigration staff to make all decisions in a conscientious and trustworthy manner. The government must emphasize to the Immigration staff the need for careful planning; adequate and reliable research; and accountability for any strategies, methods, or new laws concerning immigration reform.

America would have to offer a fair, easy, and meaningful legal immigration and citizenship process to all legal immigrants. Prior to being deported, at-risk illegal immigrants would be provided with informational pamphlets or periodicals detailing the benefits of the legal entry process and the risks of entering our country illegally. All repeat illegal immigrants could be introduced to a new law that has something in common with one of America's favorite sports: three strikes and you're out! Under this simple law, any illegal repeat offender caught three or more times would forever lose the right to enter America legally and could never apply for resident alien status or citizenship. The only way illegal repeat offenders might escape this unfortunate law would be to agree to train as a border guard and serve the U.S. government on the Mexican side of the border. As a border guard, he or she could earn American money while obeying all U.S. laws and policies. Border guards could combat the ongoing illegal drug trade and the hundreds of repeat illegal aliens.

America must put the Responsible Principle of the new immigration reform program back into the hands of illegal repeat offenders, thus making them accountable for their own actions. The Responsible Principle could provide a more efficient homeland security program by providing sufficient manpower to protect the significance of our borders and assure a safe America for all.

*The Rational Principle of the Five "R" Immigration Reform Program would have to be based on reason and logic, rather than emotion and prejudice. "For too long, politicians in Washington have exploited the immigration issue to divide the nation rather than find real solutions," states Change.gov. "Our broken immigration system can only be fixed by putting politics aside and offering a complete solution that secures our borders, enforces our laws, and reaffirms our heritage as a nation of immigrants." The new program must be sensible, governed by good judgment, and outlined in simple and easy to understand terms. The new program must strengthen our country and its borders by continuing to provide the appropriate manpower and the implements necessary to divert, cease, and punish any and all acts of terrorism and illegal activity … yet must maintain a sense of compassion through education. America is a nation of immigrants. Our cultural diversity has served to enrich and strengthen the greatest country in the world.

I will end the section of my book on Immigration Reform by quoting a statement that President Barack Obama made as a senator on the U.S. Senate Floor on May 23, 2007. I agree wholeheartedly with his statement:

> "The time to fix our broken immigration system is now ... We need stronger enforcement on the border and at the workplace ... But for reform to work, we also must respond to what pulls people to America ... Where we can unite families, we should; where we can bring in more foreign-born workers with the skills our economy needs, we should."

JULY 1958

The author (second from left) and her siblings at the Rustler Springs Ranch-1958.

MAY GOD CONTINUE TO BLESS AMERICA

America's purple mountain majesty mirrors an image of great human sacrifice with a diversity of contributions. Hard labor, determination, and skilled efforts by a kaleidoscope of immigrants from around the world are responsible for our 'Land of the Free and Home of the Brave.' Immigrants are the reason for the rich colorful history of the United States of America. May God continue to bless America in every way.

Maria Luisa Miranda

U.S. IMMIGRATION HISTORICAL LANDMARKS RESEARCHED AND CONDENSED BY M.L.M. (1795-2010)

1795

Naturalization Act restricts citizenship to 'free white persons' who live in the United States for five years and renounce their allegiance to their former country.

1798

The Alien and Sedition Acts permit the President to deport any foreigner viewed as dangerous. A revised Naturalization Act executes a 14-year residency requirement for prospective citizens.

1802

Congress decreases the residency requirement for citizenship to five years.

1808

The introduction of slaves into the United States is now prohibited.

1830

Congress passes the Removal Act, which forced Native Americans to settle Indian Territory west of the Mississippi River.

1831

Pennsylvania allows bilingual instruction in English and German in its public schools.

1838

Cherokee Indians forced on thousand mile march to the established Indian Territory. An estimated 4,000 Cherokees die on the 'Trail of Tears.'

1840s

Irish Potato Famine; crop failures in Germany; the start of industrialization; failed European revolutions begin a period of mass immigration.

1848

Treaty of Guadalupe Hidalgo, ending the Mexican War; extends citizenship to approx. 80,000 Mexican residents of the Southwest. U.S. acquires additional territory under its jurisdiction.

1849

California Gold Rush provokes mass immigration from China.

1850s

Know Nothing political party failed to increase restrictions on naturalization.

1854

Chinese immigrants are forbidden from testifying against whites in all California courts.

1870

Naturalization Act limits American citizenship to 'white persons and persons of African descent,' restricting Asians from U.S. citizenship.

1875

Supreme Court declares that regulation of U.S. immigration is the responsibility of the Federal Gov.

1882

Chinese Exclusion Act restricts Chinese immigration under penalty of imprisonment and deportation.

*Immigration Act levies a tax of 50 cents per immigrant; makes several categories of immigrants ineligible to enter the United States; including 'lunatics' and people likely to become public charges.

1885

Alien Contract Labor Law bars prohibited any company or individual from bringing foreigners into the United States under contract to perform labor here; only exceptions are those brought here to perform domestic service and skilled workmen needed to help establish some new trade or industry.

1891

Congress marks polygamists, 'persons suffering from a loathsome or a dangerous contagious disease,' and those convicted of 'a misdemeanor involving moral turpitude' ineligible for immigration. The act establishes the Bureau of Immigration within the Treasury Dept.

1892

Ellis Island opens; is processing center for 12 million immigrants for the next 30 years.

1901

After President William McKinley is assassinated by a Polish anarchist; Congress ordains the Anarchist Exclusion Act - all immigrants to be excluded on the basis of their political opinions.

1907

Expatriation Act declares that any American woman who marries a foreign national forfeits her citizenship.

1913

California's Alien Land Law prohibits 'aliens ineligible for citizenship' (Chinese and Japanese) from owning property in the state; presents the model for similar acts in other states.

1917

Congress authorizes a literacy requirement for immigrants over President Woodrow Wilson's veto; law requires immigrants to be able to read 40 words in some language. The law also indicates that immigration is prohibited from Asia, except from Japan and the Philippines.

1921

Quota Act restricts annual European Immigration to 3 % of the number of a nationality group in the United States in 1910.

1922

Cable Act partially rescinds the Expatriation Act; affirms that any American who marries an Asian still loses her citizenship.

1923

The landmark case of United States v. Bhaghat Singh Thind, the Supreme Court rules that Indians from the Asian subcontinent are prevented to become naturalized U.S. citizens.

1924

The Johnson-Reed Act limits annual European immigration to 2% of the number of nationality group in the United States in 1890.

Oriental Exclusion Act bans most immigration from Asia, including foreign-born wives/children of U.S. citizens of Chinese ancestry.

1934

The Tydings-McDuffie Act, which granted independence for the Philippines on July 4, 1946, deprives Filipinos of their status as U.S. nationals and severely limits Filipino immigration- annual immigration quota of 50.

1940

The Alien Registration Act requires the registration and fingerprinting of all aliens in the United States over the age of 14; it classifies Korean immigrants as citizens of Japan.

1942

Filipinos are reclassified as U.S. citizens; its now possible for them to register for the military.

Executive Order 9066 authorizes the military to evacuate 112,000 Japanese Americans from the Pacific coast and locate them in tent internment camps.

1943

The Chinese Exclusion Act is annulled. By the end of the 1940s, restrictions on Asians acquiring U.S. citizenship are abolished.

Congress initiates a guest worker program-The Bracero Program, brought temporary agricultural workers into the United States from Mexico. The program expired in 1964.

1944

United States vs. Korematsu, the Supreme Court sustains the interment of Japanese Americans as constitutional.

1945

The War Brides Act permits foreign-born wives of U.S. citizens who have served in the U.S. armed forces to enter the United States.

1946

Fiancés of American soldiers are admitted to enter the United States.

The Luce-Cellar Act encompasses the right to become naturalized citizens to Filipinos and Asian Indians-quota is 100 people a year.

1948

The Displaced Persons Act permits Europeans ousted by war to enter the United States outside of immigration quotas.

1950

The Internal Security Act, approved over President Harry Truman's veto, bars admission to any foreigner who is a Communist/ or who might engage in activities 'which would be prejudicial to the public interest or would endanger the welfare or safety of the United States.'

1952

McCarran Walter Immigration Act, approved over Harry Truman's veto affirms the national-origins quota system of 1924. It maximizes the total annual immigration to one-sixth of one percent of the population of the continental United States in 1920. The act frees spouses/children of U.S. citizens and people born in the Western Hemisphere from the quota.

1953

Refugee Relief Act prolongs refugee status to non-Europeans.

1954

'Operation Wetback' calls for the return of undocumented workers to Mexico.

Ellis Island closes; creates an end to mass immigration.

1965

Immigration and Nationality Act repeals the national origins quota system- focuses priority on family reunification.

Immigration Act causes immigration increase from Asia and West Indies.

1980

Refugee Act, enacted in reply to the 'boat people' fleeing Vietnam; grants asylum to politically oppressed refugees.

1986

The Immigration and Control Act gives amnesty to an estimated three million undocumented residents; forbids hiring of illegal immigrants- endows punishment for employers who hire undocumented workers.

1988

The Redress Act provides $20,000 compensation- presidential apology- to survivors of World War II internment of Japanese and Japanese Americans.

1990

The Immigration Act- intensifies the number of immigrants allowed into the United States each year to 700,000.

1995

California enacts Proposition 187-later proclaimed unconstitutional; which disallows public education, welfare, and health services to all undocumented workers.

1996

The Illegal Immigration Reform and Immigrant Responsibility Act strengthens border enforcement by sending U.S. military personnel to borders to assist existing border patrol; makes it more difficult to receive asylum. The law launches income requirements for sponsors of legal immigrants.

The Personal Responsibility and Work Opportunity Act-

Congress marks citizenship as a condition of eligibility for public benefits of illegal immigrants.

1997

Congress returns benefits for some elderly and indigent immigrants who had formerly received them.

1998

The Agricultural Research/ Extension and Education Reform Act, the Non-citizen Benefit Clarification and Other Technical Amendments Act reinstate more public benefits for some immigrants.

The American Competitiveness and Work force Improvement Act expands the number of skilled temporary foreign workers that U.S. employers are permitted to bring into America.

2001

USA Patriot Act unites and strengthens America by furnishing the appropriate tools necessary to intercept and obstruct terrorism.

2003

USCIS 2003-U.S. Immigration and Naturalization Service is now a division of the Dept. of Homeland Security. The purpose of U.S. Citizenship and Immigration Services is to operate U.S. immigration services and benefits, citizenship, applications for permanent residence, non-immigrant applications, asylum, and all refugee services. U.S. immigration enforcement roles are now under the Border and Transportation Security Directorate, known as the Bureau of U. S. Immigration and Customs Enforcement (HICE).

2006

President George W. Bush deploys U.S. military to borders across America to serve as a component of the U. S. Department of Homeland Security.

2007

Senator John Kerry, D-Massachusetts, introduced the HIV Nondiscrimination in Travel and Immigration Act; legislation that would remove a provision from the Immigration and Nationality Act that prohibits individuals with HIV from being admissible to the U.S.

2008

Immigrants who file for Naturalization on or after Oct. 1, 2008, will be required to take the new (redesigned) citizenship test. For those immigrants who file prior to Oct. 1, 2008 but are not interviewed until after October, 2008 (but before Oct. 1, 2009) there will be option of taking either test.

2009

Children's Health Insurance Reauthorization Act-

CHIPRA provides states with the option to eliminate the five year waiting period imposed on lawfully residing immigrant children and pregnant women in Medicaid and CHIP.

Rep. Sheila Jackson-Lee, D-Texas, introduced the 'Save America Comprehensive Immigration Act' (H.R. 264) that would amend the Immigration and Nationality Act to comprehensively reform immigration law.

2010

Immigration Reform-

President Barack Obama is committed to pursuing comprehensive immigration reform; a reform system in which America can have stronger border security and an orderly process by which legal immigrants can come into the United States.

Homeland Security Secretary Janet Napolitano announces streamlined citizenship application process for members of U.S. military.